cooking the
South American
way

Empanadas, or turnovers, are popular in several South American countries. (Recipe is on page 28.) They are served here with chicken rice soup (recipe on page 22) and a mixed green salad (recipe on page 24).

cooking the
South
American way

HELGA PARNELL

PHOTOGRAPHS BY ROBERT L. AND DIANE WOLFE

easy menu
ethnic
cookbooks

Lerner Publications Company ▪ Minneapolis

Editor: Mary Winget

Acknowledgments

A special thanks to Roxanne Sullivan of the Trade Winds in St. Paul, Minnesota, for the use of the South American fabrics and other props used in the photos, to Lori Schatschneider and Roma Hoff for their services as consultants, and to LeeAnne Engfer and Susan Rose for their generous assistance.

The page border for this book is based on an Indian pattern found in an Ecuadoran wall hanging. The Indians are descendants of the Incas, and the Inca influence can be seen in the small figures and geometric designs of the border.

Photographs on the following pages courtesy of: Jim Cron, p. 9; Nigel Harvey, p. 10; Amandus Schneider, p. 11; Minneapolis Public Library, p. 12; L. Nelson, p. 14.

Library of Congress Cataloging-in-Publication Data

Parnell, Helga.
   Cooking the South American way / Helga Parnell ; photographs by Robert L. and Diane Wolfe
      p.   cm. — (Easy menu ethnic cookbooks)
   Includes index.
   Summary: Introduces the history, land, and food of the countries of South America, and includes recipes for such dishes as black bean casserole from Brazil, beef soup from Argentina, and almond meringue from Chile.
   ISBN 0-8225-0925-3
   1. Cookery—South America—Juvenile literature. 2. Cookery, Latin American—Juvenile literature. 3. South America—Social life and customs—Juvenile literature. [1. Cookery—South America. 2. South America—Social life and customs. 3. Cookery, Latin American.] I. Wolfe, Robert L., ill. II. Wolfe, Diane, ill. III. Title. IV. Series.
TX716.A1P42   1991
641.598—dc20
                                                         91-12769
                                                              CIP
                                                               AC

Manufactured in the United States of America

2 3 4 5 6 7 98 97 96 95 94 93

Almond meringues with fresh fruit are a light, refreshing dessert to serve after a heavy meal. (Recipe on page 43.)

CONTENTS

Caribbean Sea

Cacao

Bananas

Beef Cattle

North Pacific Ocean

North Atlantic Ocean

Bananas

Caracas

VENEZUELA

Georgetown

Rice

SURINAME

Paramaribo

COLOMBIA

Orinoco R.

GUYANA

FRENCH GUIANA

Bogotá

Rio Negro

Equator

Coffee

Quito

Amazon River

Forestry

ECUADOR

Forestry

Nuts

Bananas

Sugar Cane

Madeira River

Rice

Sugar Cane

Potatoes

PERU

Nuts

BRAZIL

Llamas

Lima

BOLIVIA

Coffee

Sheep

Beef Cattle

Cacao

Potatoes

La Paz

Brasilia

Fish

Sucre

Fish

PARAGUAY

Paraná River

Sugar Cane

Grapes

Pilcomayo

Fruit

Asunción

Soybeans

CHILE

Wheat

South Pacific Ocean

Corn

Sheep

South Atlantic Ocean

Wheat

Santiago

Buenos Aires

URUGUAY

Fish

ARGENTINA

Montevideo

Fish

Colorado River

Beef Cattle

Fruit

Wheat

Beef Cattle

Corn

SOUTH AMERICA

Sheep

Falkland Islands

Sheep

Tierra del Fuego

Drake Passage

Rain Forest

Forest

Grassy Plains

Desert

Andes Mountains

INTRODUCTION

THE LAND

South America, the fourth largest continent in the world, is composed of 12 independent countries plus the Falkland Islands and French Guiana. The continent has three main land regions: the Andes Mountains, the Central Plains, and the Eastern Highlands. The landscape throughout those regions varies greatly. In western South America, the Andes Mountains, the world's longest mountain range, stretch almost the entire length of the continent. Rain forests (*selvas*), deserts, hardwood forests, and grassy plains (*pampas*) cover other areas of the continent. Dramatic waterfalls, enormous lakes, and rocky islands are also part of the South American landscape. And water almost totally surrounds the continent—the Caribbean Sea to the north, the Atlantic Ocean to the east, the Drake Passage to the south, and the Pacific Ocean to the west.

The climate in South America also varies greatly. For example, temperatures reach 110° F (44° C) in northern Argentina, while in southern Argentina, temperatures have dropped as low as -27° F (-33° C). However, the typical range for that region is from 32 °F (0° C) in July to 60° F (16° C) in January. Because most of South America lies in the Southern Hemisphere (south of the equator) the seasons are opposite those of countries in the Northern Hemisphere. Winter begins in June and ends about September, and summer lasts from December to March.

The western region near the Andes Mountains contains large deposits of valuable minerals, including copper, gold, lead, tin, and zinc. Much of the eastern coast is also an abundant source of minerals. Brazil, Chile, and Venezuela contain especially rich mineral deposits. Although Venezuela is the leading producer of petroleum, Argentina, Brazil, Colombia, Ecuador, and Peru also have valuable oil fields. Chile, a world leader in copper mining, also has the only known deposits of sodium nitrate, which is used in making fertilizer. Peru mines copper, lead, and zinc, and Colombia mines emeralds and coal. Tin is Bolivia's most important mineral.

Forest products are important to Brazil, Argentina, Paraguay, and Bolivia. Brazilian forest products include hardwoods (such as rosewood and mahogany), latex (used in the production of rubber), coconuts, Brazil nuts, and dates. Argentina harvests quebracho trees, which are used for telephone poles and railroad ties. The quebracho is also a source of tannin, a chemical used to make leather.

Argentina, Brazil, and Chile are the leading industrial countries in South America. Brazil produces cars, trucks, computers, televisions, and light airplanes. Argentine and Chilean industries include meat-packing and other food processing companies as well as the production of transportation equipment (such as automobiles and railroad cars), metal products, chemicals, electrical equipment, and textiles. In addition, Chilean factories produce such consumer goods as beverages, clothing, textiles, and wood products. Chile and Peru also have significant fishing industries.

Although most of the land in South America could be used for agriculture, only about one-third actually is used. Argentina and Brazil have some of the largest farms in the world —including a few that are bigger than some countries. The large farms produce such valu-able exports as bananas, coffee, grains (such as wheat, barley, and rye), soybeans, sugarcane, beef, and wool. Other agricultural exports include grapes, citrus fruits (such as oranges), corn, cacao, potatoes, and cotton. Most South American farms, however, are small, and the majority of farmers struggle to provide enough food for their families.

THE PEOPLE

The people of South America vary almost as much as the land and climate. Indians had lived on the continent for thousands of years before the Spanish and Portuguese arrived in the 16th century. The Spanish conquered the Indians and gradually took over most of South America, except for Brazil, which was ruled by Portugal. As a result, Spanish is the official language of most of South America. Exceptions include Brazil, where Portuguese is the official language; Peru and Bolivia, where Indian languages have been made official languages in addition to Spanish; Suriname, where Dutch is the official language; and Guyana, where English is the official language. (However,

Sugar Loaf Mountain dwarfs the skyscraper-apartment buildings in this suburb of Rio de Janeiro, Brazil. Because of its beautiful scenery and location, this section of Rio is one of the most densely populated parts of Brazil.

most people in Suriname and Guyana speak Creolese—a common dialect based on several local languages.)

Over the years, people from many different European countries settled in South America

This young woman is cutting sweet corn and alfalfa. Her family will eat the corn for dinner, and the family's cows will eat the alfalfa.

and frequently married Indians. Their descendants, of mixed ancestry, are called *mestizos*. Today, in most South American countries, very few Indians of unmixed ancestry still exist. In Brazil, for example, Indians make up less than 1 percent of the population. Only Peru and Bolivia have large Indian populations. Throughout most of South America, Indians live primarily in remote regions, much as their early ancestors did. Black people arrived on the continent in the 17th century, when European settlers brought them from Africa to work as slaves on large plantations.

Almost all South American countries have a rather rigid class system based on ancestry, wealth, or a combination of both. Bolivia, where mestizos belong to all classes, is an exception. Venezuela also has an open society, and people there are not segregated on the basis of race or class. Throughout South America, there is a small upper class, a growing middle class, and a very large lower class. Most people live in cities that have glass and steel skyscrapers and look much like the cities of North America. The upper and middle classes usually live in modern apartment buildings or private homes.

Much of Chile's land is mountainous. The snowcapped Andes Mountains stretch the length of the South American continent and form Chile's border with Argentina.

However, the urban poor live in crowded slums. Opportunities for education and economic development vary from country to country.

City dwellers wear clothing similar to that worn in the United States, Canada, and Europe, but some rural people wear distinctive clothing. For example, black women in northeastern Brazil wear long, colorful skirts, bright blouses, and many bracelets and necklaces. Argentine and Chilean cowboys, known as *gauchos*, wear

In Argentina's wide plains—called pampas—gauchos (South American cowboys) demonstrate their skill with horses.

a traditional costume that includes a wide-brimmed hat, a poncho (a blanket with a slit cut in it for the head), and baggy trousers tucked into low boots.

THE FOOD

If you were to travel throughout South America, you would probably find some similarities in food among the different countries, but you would also find some foods that are unique to certain countries or regions. What people eat depends in large part on what's available to them. People living in South American cities usually enjoy a much wider choice of food than those living in rural areas. In large cities, cola drinks and hamburgers are becoming as popular as they are in the United States. But in rural areas and in the poor sections of cities, beans and such foods as potatoes, rice, corn, and a starchy root called *cassava* or *manioc* still form the basic diet.

In Brazil, Argentina, Uruguay, and Paraguay, people eat large amounts of meat, especially beef. In southern Brazil, *churrasco*—a selection of charcoal-broiled meats—is a popular meal. The national dish, however, is *feijoada*—a combination of black beans, sausage, and pork. Coffee is Brazil's chief drink, but people also drink *mate*, a tealike beverage made from the dried leaves of the holly tree. In Argentina, Uruguay, and Paraguay, mate is the native drink.

Like many Brazilians, Argentines also enjoy *asados* (barbecues). Most Argentine people eat well, and beef is often eaten at all three meals. Most Argentines prefer it to lamb, fish, or chicken. Italian immigrants introduced spaghetti, lasagna, and other pastas to both the Argentine and the Uruguayan diet. And the British introduced teatime—a custom that is popular in Argentina and in several other South American countries. It is a time when people pause during a busy day to enjoy a cup of tea and a snack.

Puchero, made with meat and vegetables, is a favorite meal in Argentina as well as Chile, Paraguay, and Bolivia. *Empanadas* (pastries stuffed with meat, seafood, eggs, vegetables, or fruit) are popular in Argentina, Chile, Ecuador, and Bolivia. They are often sold along the roadside. In Uruguay *parrillada criolla* (a mixture of barbecued sausages, kidneys, and strips of beef) is well liked.

Indians in Peru are believed to have been the first people to cultivate the potato, which grew wild in the highlands. Potatoes were an important part of the Peruvian diet long before they were known anywhere else. At the present time in Peru, the upper and middle classes enjoy a varied diet of meat, fish, poultry, vegetables, and cereal products. Most Peruvians prefer food that is highly seasoned with onions and hot peppers. Usually, rice, potatoes, and bread are also served at meals.

In Colombia diets vary from region to region, but they generally consist of starchy foods such as potatoes, rice, and noodles. Stews and thick soups are popular, as is *agua de panela*, a drink made of brown sugar and water. Although Colombia is a leading producer of coffee, Colombians do not drink as much of the beverage as people in the United States do.

Potatoes, corn, and a grain called *quinoa* are among the traditional foods of Bolivia. *Humitas* (made with fresh corn) and *saltenas* (meat turnovers) are also common.

Traditional Venezuelan food includes black beans, plantains (a type of banana), and rice, which is usually eaten with beef, pork, poultry, or fish. *Arepa*, a round cornmeal cake, is the traditional bread.

Ecuadorans generally like fried foods, and *coladas* (thick meat or vegetable soups) are enjoyed in both Ecuador and Chile. *Cazuela de*

This busy local market in Peru offers shoppers a wide variety of fresh fruit.

ave, which combines meat and vegetables, is popular in Chile, but the Chilean diet is based primarily on bread, beans, and potatoes. Coffee and tea, especially an herb tea called *agüita*, are popular beverages in Chile.

In Suriname and Guyana, many ethnic groups have contributed foods that have become a regular part of the diet. In Guyana, English roast beef, puddings, and tea appear with Indian curries, Chinese noodles, and Portuguese garlic pork. The people of Suriname are also fond of a variety of foods, most of which are highly spiced. The national dish is a thick pea soup made with sausages and potatoes.

The recipes in this cookbook represent a wide variety of South American foods, but smaller amounts of herbs and spices have been used. If you prefer very spicy food, you can increase the amounts used in the recipes.

BEFORE YOU BEGIN

Cooking any dish, plain or fancy, is easier and more fun if you are familiar with its ingredients. The international dishes in this book make use of some ingredients you may not know. You should also be familiar with the special terms that will be used in these recipes. Therefore, *before* you start cooking, study the following "dictionary" of special ingredients and terms very carefully. Then read through the recipe you want to try from beginning to end.

Now you are ready to shop for ingredients and to organize the cookware you will need. Once you have assembled everything, you can begin to cook. It is also very important to read *The Careful Cook* on page 48 before you start. Following these rules will make your cooking experience safe, fun, and easy.

COOKING UTENSILS

colander – A bowl with holes in the bottom and sides. It is used for draining liquid from a solid food.

Dutch oven – A heavy pot with a tight-fitting, domed lid that is often used for cooking soups or stews

rolling pin – A cylindrical tool used for rolling out dough

slotted spoon – A spoon with small openings in its bowl. It is used to pick solid food out of a liquid.

stock pot – A large pot in which stock, or broth, is prepared as a basis for soup

COOKING TERMS

beat – To stir rapidly in a circular motion

blanch – To scald, steam, or boil briefly in water

blend – To thoroughly combine, or mix, two or more ingredients

boil – To heat a liquid over high heat until bubbles form and rise rapidly to the surface

brown – To cook food quickly over high heat so that the surface browns evenly

cream – To beat two or more ingredients together until the mixture is smooth

dice – To chop food into small, square pieces

fold – To blend an ingredient with other ingredients by using a gentle, overturning circular motion instead of by stirring or beating

grate – To cut into tiny pieces by rubbing food against a grater

ladle – To dip into and serve foods, especially such liquids as soups, gravies, and sauces, with a long-handled, deep-bowled spoon

marinate – To soak food in a seasoned liquid in order to add flavor and to tenderize it

mince – To chop food into very small pieces

preheat – To allow an oven to warm up to a certain temperature before putting food in it

puree – To make a paste or thick liquid from finely ground food

sauté – To fry quickly in oil or fat, over high heat, stirring or turning the food to prevent burning

sift – To mix several dry ingredients together or to remove lumps in dry ingredients by putting them through a sieve or sifter

simmer – To cook over low heat in liquid kept just below its boiling point. Bubbles may occasionally rise to the surface.

steam – To cook food with the steam from boiling water

stir-fry – To quickly cook bite-sized pieces of food in a small amount of oil over high heat

SPECIAL INGREDIENTS

allspice – The berry, used whole or ground, of a West Indian tree. Its flavor resembles a combination of cinnamon, nutmeg, and cloves.

avocado – The pulpy green or purple fruit of various tropical trees of the laurel family

baking powder – A powder used as a leavening agent in baked goods to make the dough or batter lighter

basil – A rich, fragrant herb whose fresh or dried leaves are used in cooking

bay leaf—The dried leaf of the bay (also called laurel) tree. It is used to season food.

blue cheese—A sharp-tasting cheese with bluish green veins running through it

bouillon— A mixture of spices, seasoning, and meat used to make broth and to add flavor to other foods

chives—A member of the onion family. The thin green stalks are chopped and used as a flavoring and as a garnish.

cilantro—The leaves of coriander, a sharp-flavored herb used as a seasoning and as a garnish

cinnamon—A spice made from the bark of a tree in the laurel family. It is available ground and in sticks.

cornstarch—A fine, white starch made from corn, commonly used for thickening sauces and gravies

cumin—The seeds of an herb used whole or ground to give food a pungent, slightly hot flavor

garlic—A bulbous herb whose distinctive flavor is used in many dishes. The bulb can be broken into several small sections called cloves. Before chopping a garlic clove, remove its papery skin.

kale—A hardy, curled-leaf cabbage that does not form a dense head

lemon extract—A liquid made from lemons that is used to flavor foods

mace—An aromatic spice made from the fibrous covering of a nutmeg

olive oil—An oil made from pressed olives. It is used in cooking and for salad dressings.

oregano—The dried leaves, whole or ground, of a rich and fragrant herb that is used as a seasoning in cooking

paprika—A red seasoning made from the ground, dried pods of the capsicum pepper plant

white wine vinegar—A vinegar made from white wine

Worcestershire sauce—A pungent sauce whose ingredients include soy, vinegar, and garlic

zucchini—A summer squash with a smooth, dark green skin. It is long and cylindrical in shape.

A SOUTH AMERICAN MENU

Below is a menu plan that offers a variety of South American food both for typical, everyday meals and for special holiday meals. Several alternatives are provided for each stage of the meal. The ethnic names of the dishes are given, along with a guide on how to pronounce them.

Soups and Stews		
Chicken Rice Soup	Canja com Arroz KAH-zhah kou ah-ROZH	Brazil
Fish Soup	Sopa de Pescado SOH-pah day pes-CAH-doh	Chile
Beef Stew	Guiso de Vacuno GEE-so day bah-KOO-noh	Peru
Beef Soup	Puchero poo-CHEH-roh	Argentina
Salads		
Mixed Green Salad	Ensalada Mixta ehn-sah-LAH-dah MEEX-tah	Chile
Vegetable Salad Platter	Ensalada de Legumbres ehn-sah-LAH-dah day leh-GOOM-brays	Chile
Seafood Salad	Ensalada de Mariscos ehn-sah-LAH-dah day mah-REES-kohs	Chile
Main Dishes		
Breaded Beef Cutlets	Milanesas mee-lah-NAY-sahs	Argentina
Turnovers	Empadas/Empanadas em-PAH-dahs/ em-pah-NAH-dahs	Brazil, Argentina, Ecuador, Chile
Black Bean Casserole	Feijoada fay-zhuh-AH-dah	Brazil

Charbroiled Beef with Sauce	Churrasco con Chimichurre
	shoo-RRAHZ-koh kohn
	  shee-me-SHOO-rree
		Brazil, Argentina,
		  Chile

Marinated Chicken	Pollo en Escabeche POY-yoh en es-kah-BAY-chay	Chile

Side Dishes

Peas	Guisantes gee-SAHN-tays	Argentina
Rice	Arroz ah-ROZH	Brazil
Corn Packages	Humitas oo-MEE-tahs	Chile, Bolivia, Ecuador

Teatime and Desserts

Finger Sandwiches	Bocaditos boh-kah-DEE-tohs	Argentina
Petits Fours	Masas Finas MAH-sahs FEE-nahs	Argentina
Nut Cake	Bolo de Nozes BOH-luh dih NOUZH-ehs	Brazil
Filled Cookies	Alfajores ahl-fah-HO-rays	Argentina
Sweet Treats/Dark and Light	Negrinho y Brouquinho nay-GREE-nyuh brow-KEE-nyuh	Brazil

Milk Pudding (Flan)	Dulce de Leche, Pudim
	  de Leite
	DOOL-thay day LAY-che
	  poo-DIH dih LAY-teh
		Brazil, Argentina

Almond Meringues with
Fresh Fruit
	Merengues de Almendra
	  con Frutas Frescas
	meh-REN-gays day ahl-MEN-drah
	  kohn FROO-tahs FRES-kahs
		Chile

SOUPS and STEWS

The soups below are a good way to begin dinner. Served with fresh, warm bread, they also make a hearty and nourishing lunch.

Fish Soup/
Sopa de Pescado
Chile

Chilean sea bass is a popular variety of fish for use in this recipe and many others. Since sea bass may not always be available, any other type of white fish, such as cod, can be substituted.

1 to 1½ pounds cod or other white fish, cut into bite-sized pieces
1 large onion, peeled and chopped
2 medium tomatoes, peeled and seeded
1 medium potato, peeled and diced
1 small carrot, sliced
½ lemon, cut into slices
1 bay leaf
3 cups water
4 sprigs parsley or dill

1. Combine all ingredients in a large saucepan or stock pot and bring to a boil.
2. Reduce heat and simmer for 30 minutes, until fish is well done.
3. Remove lemon slices and bay leaf. Garnish soup with fresh parsley or dill, and serve hot with crusty bread.

Serves 4

Beef Soup/
Puchero
Argentina

1½ **pounds beef (shoulder, rump, or flank steak)**
1 **tablespoon vegetable oil**
6 **cups water**
2 **teaspoons salt**
½ **teaspoon pepper**
4 **small, whole potatoes, peeled**
3 **carrots, peeled and each cut into 6 pieces**
8 **pearl onions**
½ **pound whole green beans, tips and strings removed**
2 **stalks celery, cut in bite-sized pieces**
6 **sprigs parsley or cilantro**

1. Cut meat into bite-sized pieces.
2. In large saucepan or Dutch oven, brown meat lightly in vegetable oil.
3. Add water, salt, and pepper, and bring mixture to a boil.
4. Reduce heat, cover, and simmer for 1½ hours or until meat is tender.
5. Add vegetables, cover, and simmer for 30 minutes.
6. Remove meat and vegetables from broth, arrange them on a platter, and keep warm. Before serving, garnish with parsley or cilantro.
7. Ladle broth into 4 soup bowls, garnish with chopped parsley, or cilantro and serve.

Serves 4

Crusty bread complements fish soup (recipe on page 20) from Chile and beef stew (background) from Peru.

Chicken Rice Soup/
Canja com Arroz
Brazil

1 frying chicken, cut into pieces
2 stalks celery with leaves, cut in
    4 pieces
1 carrot, peeled and cut in 4 pieces
1 onion, peeled and quartered
    stems from one bunch of parsley
2 teaspoons salt
¼ teaspoon pepper
8 cups water

1. Place all ingredients in large saucepan or stock pot and bring to a boil.
2. Reduce heat, cover, and simmer for 1½ hours.
3. Using a colander, strain broth into a bowl. Set chicken pieces aside to cool. Discard cooked vegetables.
4. Return liquid to pot, and add the following ingredients:

2 stalks celery, diced
2 carrots, peeled and diced

1 medium parsnip, peeled and diced
1 medium turnip, peeled and diced
1 tomato, chopped
⅓ cup rice
¼ teaspoon basil
¼ cup chopped parsley or chives for
    garnish

5. Cover and simmer for 20 minutes.
6. When chicken is cool enough to handle, skin and bone chicken meat, then cut in small, bite-sized pieces. Add to broth and heat thoroughly.
7. Serve hot, garnished with chopped parsley or chives.

Serves 4 to 6

Beef Stew/
Guiso de Vacuno
Peru

3 tablespoons vegetable oil
2 medium onions, chopped
1½ pounds round steak, cubed
2 teaspoons paprika
1 teaspoon cumin
1 teaspoon garlic powder

¼ teaspoon red pepper flakes
1 teaspoon salt
¼ cup white wine vinegar
2 cups beef bouillon
2 cups squash, peeled and cut into
    ½-inch pieces
1 cup frozen peas
1 cup frozen corn
3 sprigs parsley

1. Heat oil in a pan and sauté onions.
2. Add meat and brown well, about 20 minutes.
3. Add all spices, the vinegar, and the beef bouillon. Bring to a boil, stirring to mix well.
4. Reduce heat, cover, and simmer about 45 minutes.
5. Add squash, cover, and simmer for 20 minutes.
6. Add peas and corn and heat thoroughly.
7. Garnish with parsley and serve.

Serves 6

SALADS

Mixed Green Salad/
Ensalada Mixta
Chile

1 head Bibb lettuce
1 head romaine lettuce
4 ripe olives (optional)
4 cherry tomatoes, quartered (optional)
¼ cup blue cheese, crumbled (optional)

1. Arrange lettuce in salad bowl.
2. Pour dressing over the lettuce and toss to coat leaves.
3. Garnish with olives, tomatoes, and cheese.

Serves 6

Vegetable Salad Platter/
Ensalada de Legumbres
Chile

4 carrots, blanched and sliced
¼ pound green beans, blanched
½ red pepper, sliced in strips
1 small zucchini, sliced
1 small cucumber, sliced
4 to 5 mushrooms, sliced
2 to 3 cherry tomatoes
2 small potatoes, cooked, peeled, and sliced
3 to 6 stalks celery, sliced in strips
6 to 8 asparagus spears, blanched

1. Arrange vegetables on a platter.
2. Pour dressing over them evenly.

Serves 8

Dressing/Aliño

½ cup olive oil
2 tablespoons lemon juice
1 large clove garlic, minced
½ teaspoon salt
¼ teaspoon pepper

1. Combine all ingredients in a small jar.
2. Cover tightly and shake well.

Makes about ½ cup

Seafood Salad/
Ensalada de Mariscos
Chile

       4 medium tomatoes
     ¼ cup mayonnaise
     ¼ cup sour cream
       1 tablespoon lemon juice
     ½ teaspoon salt
     ¼ teaspoon pepper
     ½ pound shrimp or crabmeat
       1 small head lettuce
       1 avocado, peeled and sliced
       4 sprigs parsley or cilantro
16 to 20 black olives

1. Carefully scrape out the pulpy centers of 4 tomatoes and set aside.
2. Mix mayonnaise, sour cream, lemon juice, salt, pepper, and pulp of tomatoes.
3. Add shrimp or crab, and mix well.
4. Fill the tomatoes with the seafood mixture.
5. Arrange lettuce leaves on individual plates, place filled tomatoes in center, and garnish with avocado slices, parsley or cilantro, and olives.

Serves 4

This delicately flavored seafood salad (foreground) reflects the bounty from Chile's long seacoast. The vegetable platter (rear) makes a colorful and healthy appetizer.

Breaded beef cutlets, rice, and peas are combined to create this delectable dinner. (Recipes for the rice and peas are on page 34.)

MAIN DISHES

Breaded Beef Cutlets/
Milanesas
Argentina

Beef, which is plentiful in Argentina, is the favorite meat of most Argentine people. You would find these tasty cutlets on most restaurant menus and in home cooking, served with potatoes or rice and a vegetable or salad.

¾ **cup bread crumbs**
¾ **teaspoon oregano**
¼ **cup flour**
½ **teaspoon salt**
¼ **teaspoon pepper**
1 **pound beef (eye of the round), cut
    into 8 slices**
1 **egg, beaten
    oil for frying**
4 **lemon wedges**

1. Mix bread crumbs and oregano. Set aside.
2. Mix flour, salt, and pepper.
3. Coat beef slices with flour mixture. Dip them in the beaten egg, then roll in the breadcrumbs, coating well.
4. Heat oil in large skillet, then add beef slices.
5. Cook over medium heat 4 to 5 minutes on each side, or until browned.
6. Garnish with lemon wedges before serving.

Serves 4

Turnovers/
Empadas/Empanadas
Brazil, Argentina, Ecuador, Chile

By changing the size and the filling, this versatile recipe can be used as a main dish, an appetizer, or a dessert.

Pastry
1½ cups flour
  1 teaspoon baking powder
  3 tablespoons cold butter or margarine
  2 tablespoons cooking oil
  1 teaspoon water
  3 eggs, beaten

1. Preheat oven to 400°.
2. Sift flour and baking powder into medium bowl.
3. With a pastry blender, a fork, or two knives, cut in butter and oil until coarsely blended.
4. Add water and eggs. Mix until dough holds together.

5. On a lightly floured surface, roll dough to ⅛-inch thickness.
6. Using a saucepan cover, cut 8-inch circles from dough, and place them on a lightly greased baking sheet. (Use a cookie cutter or the rim of a glass to cut 4-inch circles if the empanadas will be used as appetizers.)
7. Place ⅓ to ½ cup of your favorite filling (recipes on next page) in the center of each 8-inch circle, or 1 heaping teaspoon on the 4-inch circle.
8. Fold circles in half, moisten edges with water, and firmly press edges together with a fork.
9. Bake at 400° for 25 minutes.
   Makes 8 8-inch or 16 4-inch empanadas

Beef Filling/
Relleno de Carne Picada

½ **pound ground beef**
1 **tablespoon vegetable oil**
1 **small onion, chopped**
½ **teaspoon ground cumin**
½ **teaspoon paprika**
½ **teaspoon salt**
¼ **teaspoon pepper**
10 **green olives, sliced**
¼ **cup raisins**

1. Sauté onion in oil.
2. Add meat and brown well.
3. Add seasonings, mix well, and cook over medium heat for 20 minutes.
4. Remove from heat, add olives and raisins, and mix well.
5. Spoon onto pastry.

Chicken Filling/
Relleno de Pollo

2 **cups cooked chicken, minced**
1 **cup cream cheese with chives**
2 **tablespoons minced parsley**

Ham and Cheese Filling/
Relleno de Jamón y Queso

2 **cups chopped ham**
⅔ **cup shredded Swiss or other hard cheese**
1 **tablespoon hot sauce or Worcestershire sauce**
2 **tablespoons chopped tomato**

Fruit Filling/
Relleno de Frutas

2 **cups chopped apples**
2 **tablespoons sugar**
2 **teaspoons cinnamon**

For any of the three fillings above, mix the ingredients in a small bowl and spoon filling onto pastry circles.

Black Bean Casserole/ Feijoada
Brazil

This national dish can be varied by adding different kinds of meat, such as smoked beef tongue, smoked pork, ribs, or other cuts of pork. Feijoada is a heavy meal usually reserved for festive occasions. It is often followed by a nap.

2 cups black beans
4 cups water
1 ham bone or pork hock
1 teaspoon salt
½ teaspoon pepper
8 pork sausage links or hot dogs

1. Rinse beans thoroughly in cold water. In a large, covered pot, add enough water to cover beans. Soak overnight.
2. Drain beans and add 4 cups fresh water, ham bone or pork hock, salt, and pepper.
3. Bring to a boil, then reduce heat, cover, and simmer over low heat for 3 hours.
4. Brown pork links, cut in bite-sized pieces, and add to the bean mixture. If using hot dogs, cut them into bite-sized pieces and add directly to the bean mixture. Heat thoroughly.
5. Serve with rice and kale (recipes on page 34).

Serves 6 to 8

Black bean casserole, or *feijoada*, served with orange slices, is a filling Brazilian dish for special occasions. Kale and rice (recipes on page 34) are tasty accompaniments.

On a warm summer evening, *humitas* made with fresh sweet corn (recipe on page 35) is a nice complement to charbroiled beef basted with *chimichurri* (foreground). Marinated chicken (top) is great for picnics.

Marinated Chicken/ Pollo en Escabeche
Chile

6 pieces chicken (thighs and drumsticks)
    salt and pepper to taste
1 tablespoon vegetable oil
1 large onion, sliced
1 stalk celery, chopped
¾ cup white wine vinegar
½ cup water
½ lemon, sliced
2 bay leaves
½ teaspoon mace
¼ teaspoon allspice

1. Wash chicken thoroughly and pat dry with paper towels.
2. Sprinkle chicken with salt and pepper.
3. Heat oil in frying pan. Add chicken and brown on all sides.
4. Add all other ingredients and stir to mix.
5. Reduce heat, cover, and simmer for 30 minutes.
6. Transfer chicken to a bowl and skim fat off top of liquid remaining in frying pan.
7. Return chicken to liquid, cover, and refrigerate overnight. Serve cold.

Serves 4

Charbroiled Beef with Sauce/
Churrasco com Chimichurri
Brazil, Argentina, Chile

1½ pounds sirloin, or other steak
    suitable for barbecuing
½ cup olive or vegetable oil
½ cup cider vinegar
2 cloves garlic, crushed
1 tablespoon chopped parsley
1 teaspoon salt
½ teaspoon pepper

1. To make the chimichurri, combine all ingredients except meat.
2. Over hot coals, cook meat about 6 minutes on first side. Brush or spoon chimichurri on meat while it is cooking.
3. Turn meat, brush or spoon chimichurri on it, and cook meat for an additional 4 minutes, or until done as desired.

Serves 4

SIDE DISHES

Rice/Arroz
Brazil

¾ cup rice
1½ cups water
½ teaspoon salt

1. Combine all ingredients in saucepan.
2. Bring to a boil. Reduce heat, cover, and cook until water is absorbed, 20 to 30 minutes.

Serves 4

Peas/Guisantes
Argentina

1 tablespoon butter or margarine, melted
1 10-ounce package frozen peas
4 eggs

1. Melt butter in frying pan and sauté peas over medium heat for 5 minutes.

2. Carefully crack eggs on top of peas. Cover and steam until eggs are cooked, about 5 minutes.
3. Gently transfer to serving dish or directly onto individual plates.

Serves 4

Kale/Couve
Brazil

1 head kale
2 tablespoons olive or vegetable oil
2 cloves garlic

1. Wash kale thoroughly and remove ribs.
2. Roll each leaf and slice into thin strips.
3. Heat oil in a medium saucepan, add garlic, and sauté.
4. Add kale and stir-fry until tender but not soft, about 3 to 4 minutes.

Serves 4

Corn Packages/
Humitas
Chile, Bolivia, Ecuador

6 ears corn with husks
1 medium onion, minced
1½ teaspoons salt
1 tablespoon basil
¾ teaspoon paprika
1 tablespoon oil
2 tablespoons sugar (optional)

1. Carefully remove corn husks, rinse them well, and set aside in a pan of water.
2. With a knife, carefully remove kernels from cob by cutting down and away from you.
3. Using a blender or food processor, puree corn kernels until smooth and creamy.
4. Mix onion with salt, basil, and paprika, and stir-fry in hot oil for about 3 minutes.
5. Add the corn paste and mix well.
6. Arrange 4 to 6 corn husks so the wide ends overlap in the center. Repeat until you have 6 "packages."
7. Place 2 tablespoons of the corn mix in the middle of each husk package.

8. Fold the 2 long sides in over the corn mixture, then fold the 2 ends toward the center so the corn mixture is covered.
9. Tear strips from unused husks, and use them to tie each corn package, or *humita*, securely. String or thread can also be used.
10. Place humitas in a large kettle of boiling water. Reduce heat and simmer for 20 minutes.
11. Remove from water, drain, and serve warm. At the table, each person unwraps the humita and eats the warm corn mixture inside the husks. Some people like a little sugar sprinkled over the warm corn.

Serves 4

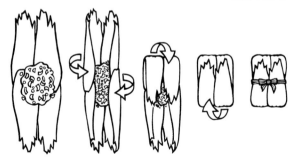

TEATIME and DESSERTS
Merienda y Postres

The British introduced teatime to Argentina. It is a custom many people observe, pausing in the late afternoon to enjoy a cup of tea and a light snack.

Petits Fours/
Masas Finas
Argentina

These dainty little cakes always make teatime a special occasion.

Cake

```
    1 cup flour
1½ teaspoons baking powder
   ¼ cup cornstarch
   ⅛ teaspoon salt
    3 eggs
    1 cup sugar
   ¼ teaspoon lemon extract or grated
        rind of ½ lemon
    5 tablespoons water
```

1. Preheat oven to 350°. Lightly grease a 9-inch square baking pan.
2. Sift together flour, baking powder, cornstarch, and salt. Set aside.
3. Beat eggs until light and creamy.
4. Add sugar to eggs, ¼ cup at a time, beating well after each addition.
5. Add lemon and water, and beat well.
6. Fold in the flour mixture a little at a time.
7. Pour batter into pan and bake for 25 to 30 minutes.
8. Remove cake from pan and cool on wire rack. When cool, slice into 16 squares.

Frosting

```
    3 cups powdered sugar
   ¾ teaspoon lemon extract
    3 tablespoons melted butter
3 to 4 tablespoons hot water
```

1. In small bowl, beat all ingredients until creamy.
2. Spread frosting evenly on top and sides of cake squares.

Serves 8

Nut cake (top, recipe on page 38), finger sandwiches (bottom left, recipe on page 38), and petits fours (bottom right) make teatime a special treat.

Finger Sandwiches/
Bocaditos
Argentina

These tiny tidbits can be as much fun to make as they are to eat. You can garnish them with almost anything you like, so use your imagination.

  12 thin slices French bread
    1 3-ounce container whipped
       cream cheese with chives
   ½ cucumber, thinly sliced
4 to 6 precooked shrimps
    4 cherry tomatoes
    4 pimento-stuffed olives, sliced

1. Trim crusts from bread.
2. Spread a thin layer of cream cheese on bread.
3. Garnish with cucumber slices, a shrimp, cherry tomatoes, or olives.

Serves 6

Nut Cake/
Bolo de Nozes
Brazil

6 eggs, separated
½ teaspoon salt
2 tablespoons cocoa
1 cup sugar
2 cups Brazil nuts, finely ground
2 tablespoons unseasoned bread
   crumbs
1 pint whipping cream

1. Preheat oven to 350°.
2. In a small bowl, combine the egg yolks, salt, cocoa, and ½ cup sugar. Beat well.
3. Mix in the ground nuts and bread crumbs.
4. In a large bowl, beat the egg whites until slightly stiff. Gradually add ½ cup sugar, beating after each addition. Continue beating until egg whites are very stiff.
5. Gently fold the egg yolk mixture into the egg whites.
6. Pour batter into 2 lightly greased 9-inch, round cake pans and bake at 350° for 35

minutes or until a toothpick inserted in the middle comes out clean.

7. Remove cakes from pans, and cool on wire racks.

8. Beat whipping cream until stiff.

9. When cake layers are completely cool, place one layer on a cake plate and frost with whipped cream. Top with the second layer and cover top and sides with remaining whipped cream. Refrigerate until ready to serve.

Serves 8 to 10

Milk Pudding (Flan)/ Dulce de Leche/ Pudim de Leite Brazil, Argentina

4 eggs
1 14-ounce can sweetened condensed milk
½ cup whole milk
⅓ cup sugar
1 T water

1. With a hand mixer or in a blender, beat eggs.

2. Add condensed and whole milk and blend well. Set custard mixture aside.

3. Heat sugar & water over medium-high heat in a small saucepan, stirring constantly, until sugar carmelizes (turns brown and syrupy).

4. Quickly pour sugar mixture into bottom of ovenproof mold or bowl, coating the bottom and sides of container.

5. Pour custard mixture into the mold.

6. Bake at 350° for 45 minutes, or until a toothpick inserted in the center comes out clean.

7. Chill until ready to serve. Turn onto platter. The pudding will be covered with a caramel sauce.

Serves 6

Milk pudding (foreground, recipe on page 39), filled cookies (top, far left and right), and sweet treats (top, center) are always welcome desserts.

Filled Cookies/
Alfajores
Argentina

These delicate cookies are favorites at teatime and at special parties.

Filling

1 14-ounce can sweetened condensed
    milk
1 tablespoon butter or margarine,
    melted
2 tablespoons lemon extract
1 cup shredded coconut

1. Fill a saucepan with enough water to cover the can of condensed milk, and bring water to a boil.
2. Submerge unopened can of condensed milk in water, reduce heat, and simmer for 3 hours.
3. Cool milk.
4. Combine milk with melted butter or margarine and lemon extract and beat until smooth. Refrigerate until ready to use.

Cookies

½ **lemon**
½ **cup flour**
 1 **teaspoon baking powder**
1¼ **cups cornstarch**
 6 **tablespoons butter**
¾ **cup sugar**
 1 **whole egg**
 1 **egg yolk**

1. Preheat oven to 350°.
2. Grate rind of lemon. Set aside.
3. Sift flour, baking powder, and cornstarch together. Set aside.
4. Cream butter and sugar until smooth. Add lemon rind, egg, and egg yolk, and continue beating.
5. Add flour mixture a little at a time and mix until dough is smooth.
6. On a lightly floured surface, roll dough to ⅛-inch thickness.
7. Using a cookie cutter or the rim of a glass, cut dough into 2-inch circles.
8. Arrange circles on baking sheet and bake at 350° for about 15 minutes.
9. Allow cookies to cool for one minute before removing from baking sheet. Cool completely on wire rack.
10. When cool, spread 1 teaspoon filling on each cookie and roll the side with topping in the coconut.
11. Place one cookie on top of another (filled sides up) to form a "sandwich."

Makes 3 dozen cookies

Sweet Treats (Chocolate)/ Negrinho
Brazil

This dessert (both versions) is a favorite at children's parties.

1 14-ounce can sweetened condensed
   milk
1 egg yolk
1 tablespoon butter or margarine
4 tablespoons sweetened cocoa
½ cup chocolate sprinkles, ground nuts,
   or shredded coconut for decoration

1. In a saucepan over low heat, combine the milk and egg yolk, stirring constantly, until the mixture thickens and coats the spoon (almost the consistency of pudding).
2. Stir in the butter or margarine and cocoa, remove from heat, and let mixture cool.
3. With wet hands, form the mixture into small balls and roll them in chocolate sprinkles, ground nuts, or shredded coconut. Store in a cool place.

Makes 3 dozen cookies

Sweet Treats (Light)/ Brouquinho

This is a variation of the previous recipe.

1 14-ounce can sweetened condensed
   milk
1 egg yolk
1 tablespoon butter or margarine
½ cup ground nuts or shredded coconut
   for decoration

1. Follow steps 1 and 2 for the recipe at left, omitting the cocoa.
2. When the mixture is cool, follow step 3 at left.

Makes 3 dozen cookies

Almond Meringues with Fresh Fruit/
Merengues de Almendra con Frutas Frescas
Chile

3 egg whites, at room temperature
¼ teaspoon cream of tartar
¾ teaspoon vanilla
pinch of salt
¾ cup sugar
¾ cup finely chopped toasted almonds
sliced fresh fruit or berries, or well-drained canned fruit of your choice

1. Cover a baking sheet with kitchen parchment paper or heavy-duty aluminum foil (dull side up).
2. Preheat the oven to 300°.
3. Beat egg whites, cream of tartar, vanilla, and salt until stiff peaks form.
4. Add the sugar, 1 tablespoon at a time, and beat well after each addition. Continue beating until the mixture, called a meringue, is stiff and glossy.
5. Gently fold in the almonds.
6. With a spoon, form 6 evenly divided mounds of meringue, about 1½ inches apart, on the lined baking sheet. Using the back of the spoon, build up the sides and make a small hollow in the center of each mound to form a nestlike shape.
7. Bake at 300° for 20 to 25 minutes. The meringues should be just starting to brown but still white and soft in the center.
8. Turn the oven off. Let the meringues cool in the oven.
9. When ready to serve, clean, peel, and slice the fruit. Place the meringues on individual plates and top them with fruit.

Serves 6

THE CAREFUL COOK

Whenever you cook, there are certain safety rules you must always keep in mind. Even experienced cooks follow these rules when they are in the kitchen.

1. Always wash your hands before handling food.
2. Thoroughly wash all raw vegetables and fruits to remove dirt, chemicals, and insecticides.
3. Use a cutting board when cutting up vegetables and fruits. Don't cut them in your hand! And be sure to cut in a direction *away* from you and your fingers.
4. Long hair or loose clothing can catch fire if brought near the burners of a stove. If you have long hair, tie it back before you start cooking.
5. Turn all pot handles away from you so that you will not catch your sleeves or jewelry on them. This is especially important when younger brothers and sisters are around. They could easily knock a pot off the stove and get burned.

6. Always use a pot holder to steady hot pots or to take pans out of the oven. Don't use a wet cloth on a hot pan because the steam this produces can burn you.
7. Lift the lid of a steaming pot with the opening away from you so that you will not get burned.
8. If you get burned, hold the burn under cold running water. Do not put grease or butter on it. Cold water helps to take the heat out, but grease or butter will only keep it in.
9. If grease or cooking oil catches fire, throw baking soda or salt at the bottom of the flame to put it out. (Water will *not* put out a grease fire.) Call for help, and try to turn all the stove burners to "off."

METRIC CONVERSION CHART

WHEN YOU KNOW		MULTIPLY BY	TO FIND	
MASS (weight)				
ounces	(oz)	28.0	grams	(g)
pounds	(lb)	0.45	kilograms	(kg)
VOLUME				
teaspoons	(tsp)	5.0	milliliters	(ml)
tablespoons	(Tbsp)	15.0	milliliters	
fluid ounces	(oz)	30.0	milliliters	
cup	(c)	0.24	liters	(l)
pint	(pt)	0.47	liters	
quart	(qt)	0.95	liters	
gallon	(gal)	3.8	liters	
TEMPERATURE				
Fahrenheit	(°F)	5/9 (after subtracting 32)	Celsius	(°C)

COMMON MEASURES AND THEIR EQUIVALENTS

3 teaspoons = 1 tablespoon

8 tablespoons = ½ cup

2 cups = 1 pint

2 pints = 1 quart

4 quarts = 1 gallon

16 ounces = 1 pound

INDEX

(recipes indicated by **bold face** *type)*

ABOUT THE AUTHOR

Helga Parnell moved from Germany to the United States in 1963. Since 1969 Parnell has managed a catering and food service business in St. Paul, Minnesota. In developing the recipes for this book, she worked with Zila Oliveira of Brazil, Stella Piazza-Ercole of Argentina, and Guillermo Moreno of Chile. Besides cooking, Parnell enjoys music, swimming, and cross-country skiing.

Beef soup, or *puchero*, is a complete meal prepared in a single pot. (Recipe on page 21.)